This book is published by
Grosvenor House Publishing Ltd
Link House
140 The Broadway, Tolworth, Surrey, KT6 7HT.
www.grosvenorhousepublishing.co.uk

A CIP record for this book
is available from the British Library

ISBN 978-1-83615-216-3

The Forest Stewardship Council™ (FSC®).
Programme for the Endorsement of Forest Certification™ (PEFC™).
The Sustainable Forestry Initiative® (SFI®).

Clementine

By

A. Shian

Grosvenor House
Publishing Limited

To my penguin,
And to Leni,
The one that made me
believe you still exist.

I wanted to paint you a picture in gold
But life gave me blue
So, I tried anyway

Your chest was my safe place to lay my head
But the salty waves came and stung my eyes

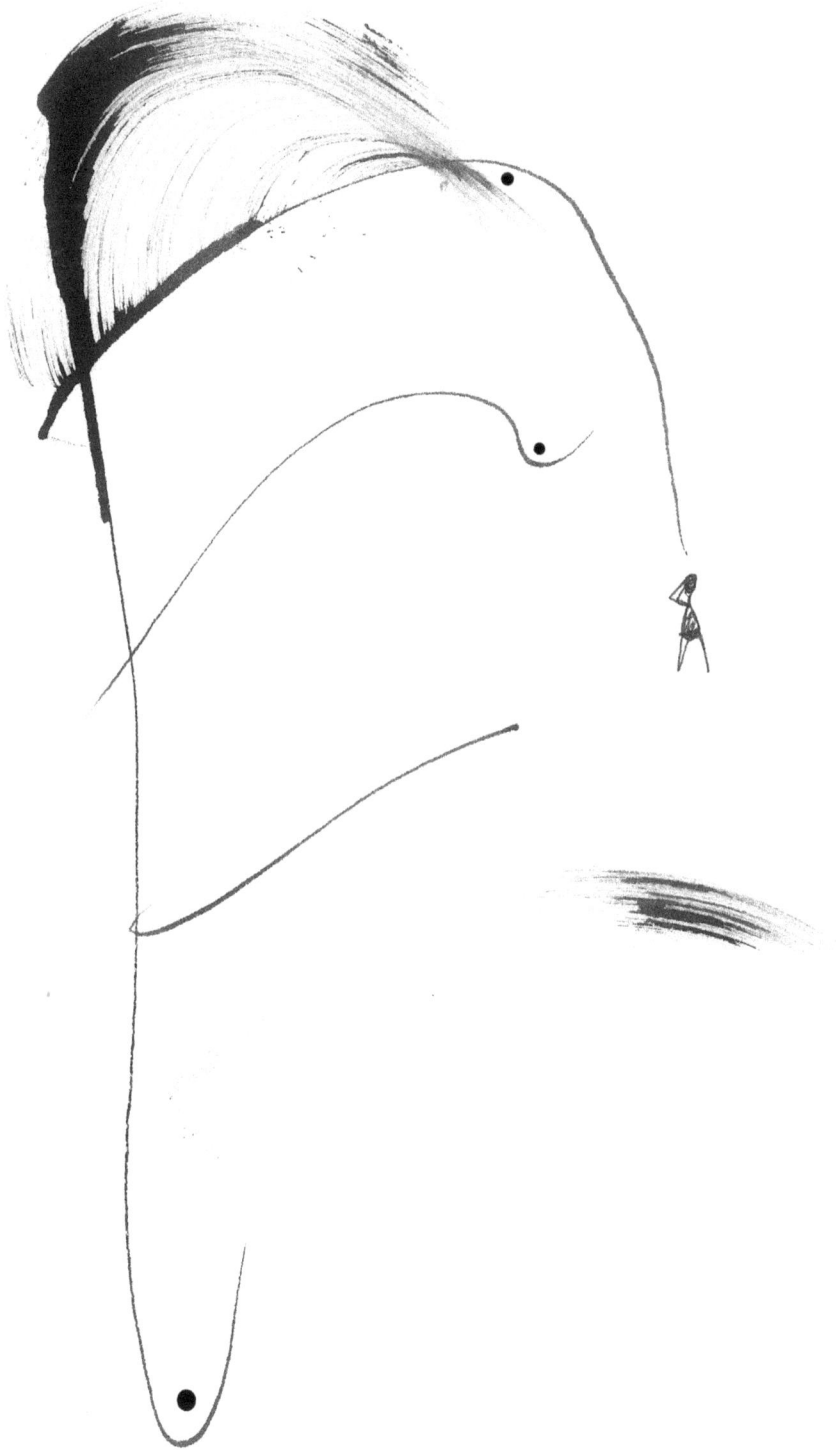

Each pebble on a beach is different
Yet there are more stars than grains of sand
Explain that to each other

My house will have a big tree in the middle
Yours would have a padded room
How opposites attract

You, Me, and a whiskey sour please

Time passes
Stains can be removed
Cables can be unfolded
But love is sticky

From one end to the other end
Beats on the road
Drive enough and you will
See where it all began

22 because it's not against the law to want you twice

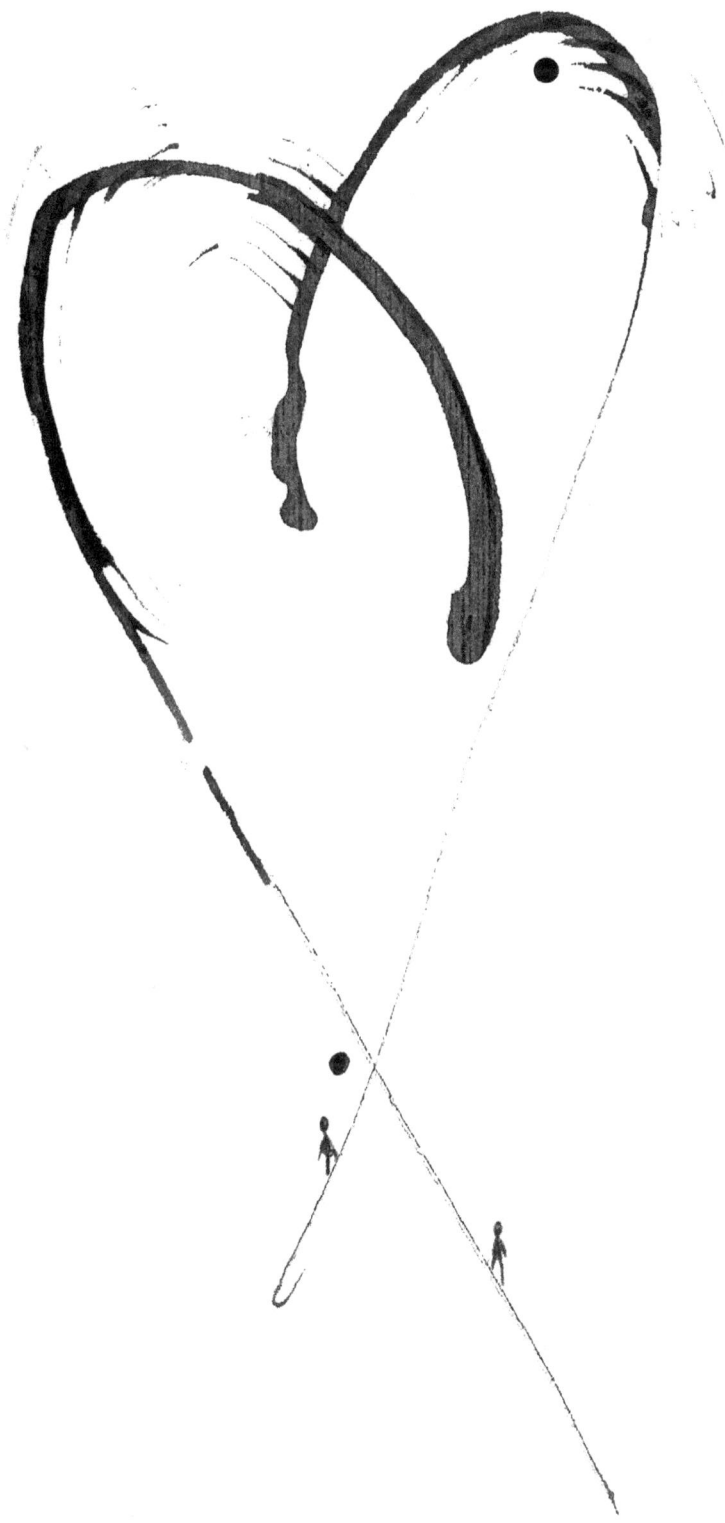

Dramatic skies
Pink and bright
All the way to the end of the pier

Guide me towards that place of ease
The one where we sit in silence
But where the hard truths are spoken

We can turn back before it is too late
Before that last autumn leaf drops
I did warn you and now we have both fallen

Make yourself at home
But don't ask me to iron your jumper

Cake is a nice gift
A rainbow one makes it magical
I took a bite out of it

You need me as much as I need you
To deny that is just foolish

If you join me and put your feet in the sand
It will not make the sun stop shining for us

Longing hurts
Hope cures

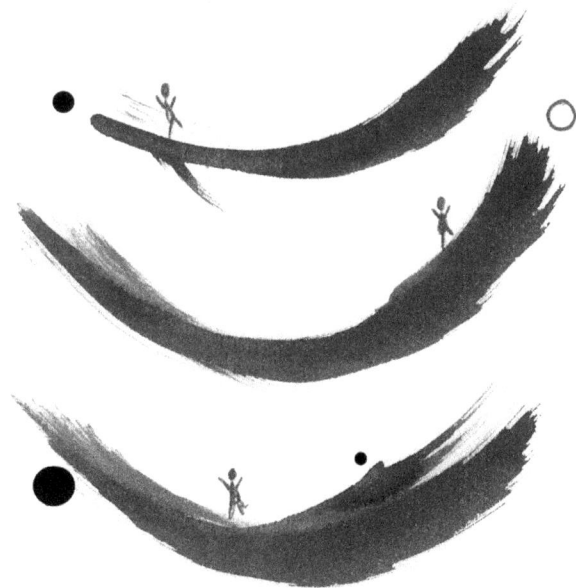

Trees need space in between them to grow
The soil becomes weak
And I slowly slip away

Coffee makes it easier to decide
Make it bitter and it leaves you heartbroken

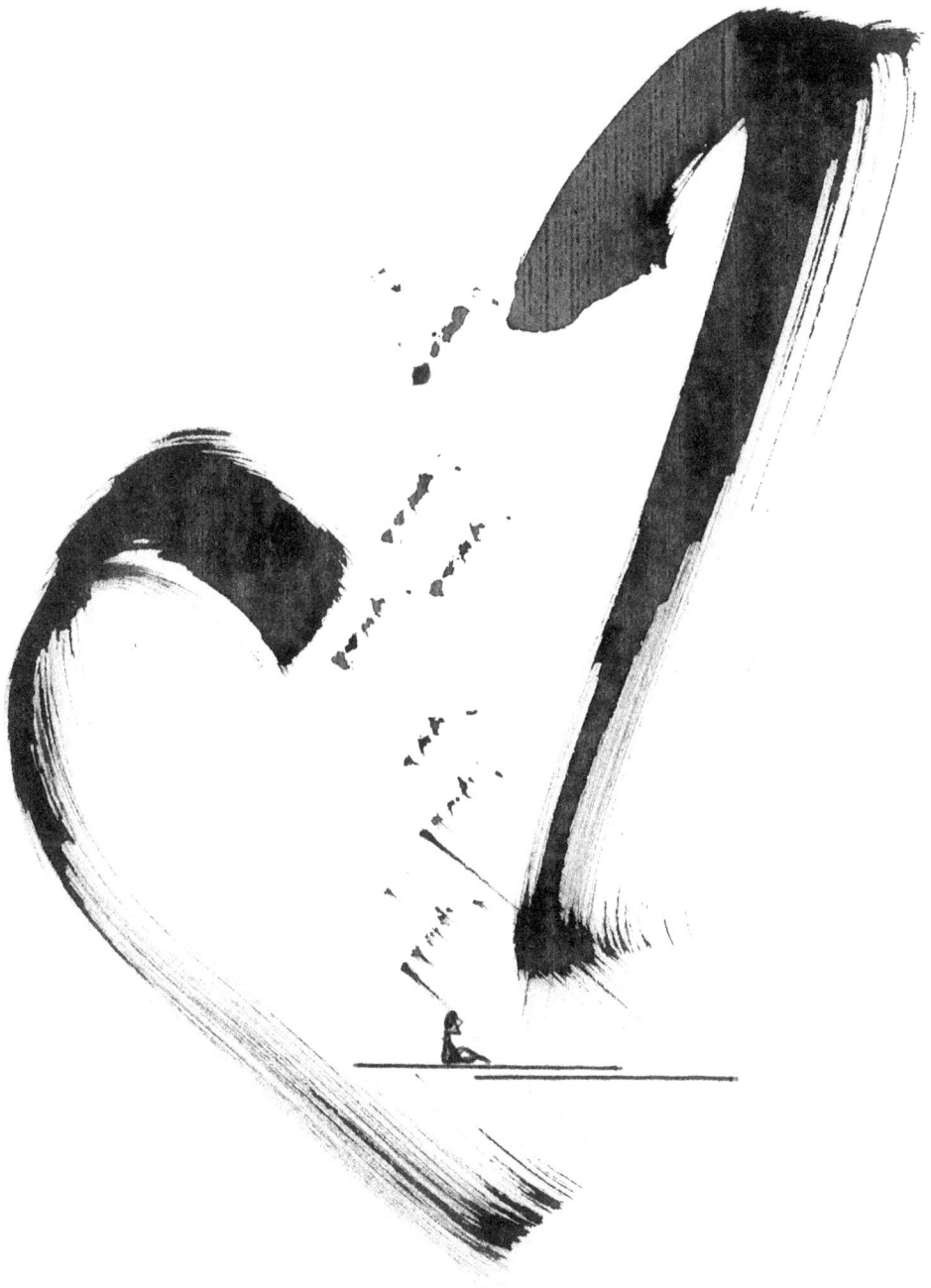

I looked and dreamt to find you
By closing my eyes, I felt you
By opening them, I lost you

Our hands just fit
Without judgement

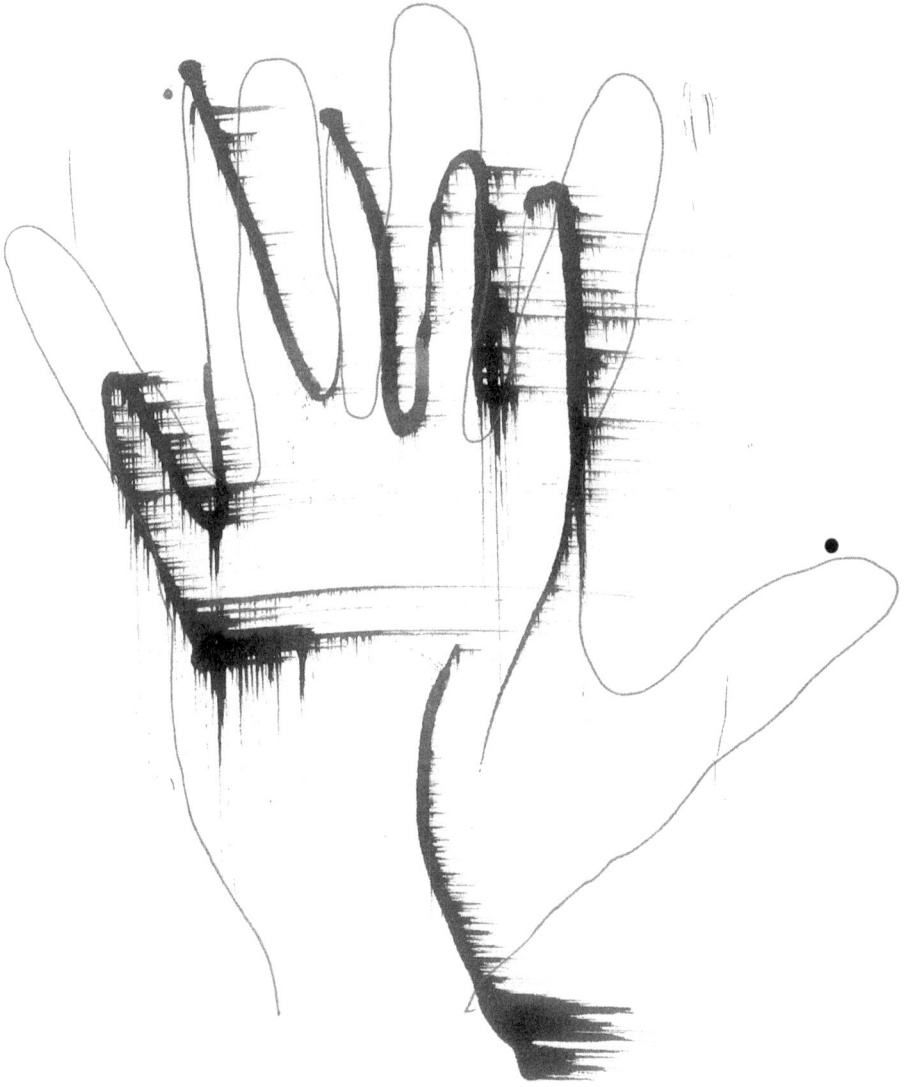

With one look of your eye
It's September again
And we need to dance

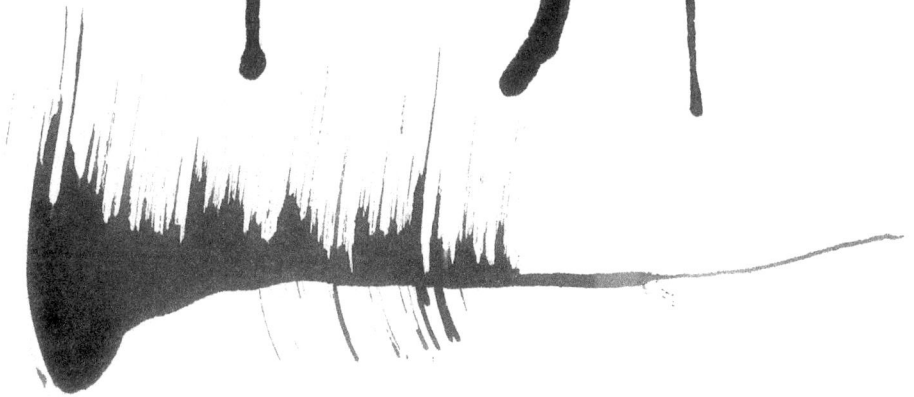

Mates in one life
Strangers in another
So, when did our souls meet

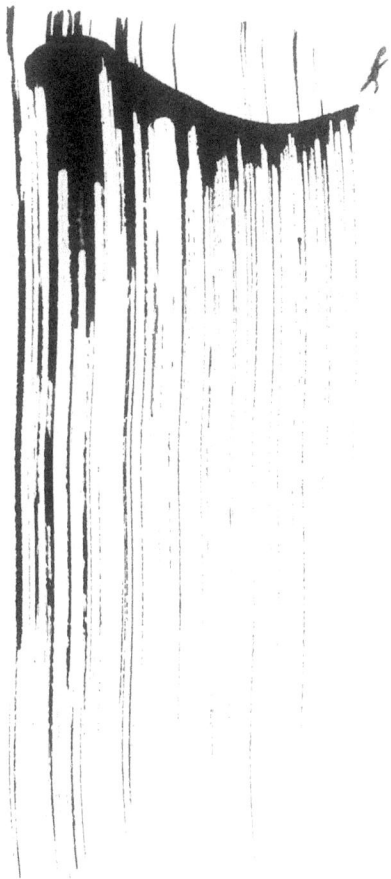

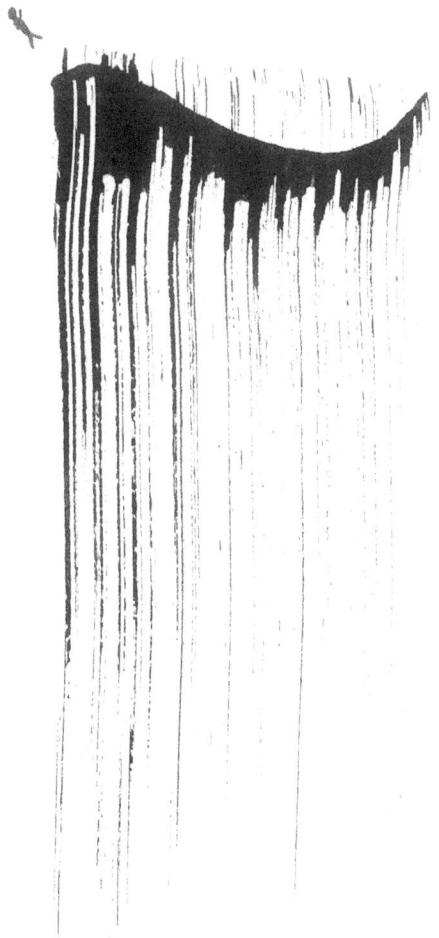

To hold my hand makes your chest tight
To look at me haunts you
To have me will save us both

Don't do that again
Do that again
Said at the same time means
More than that again

Love of my life
I have not forgotten
Nor will those above let me

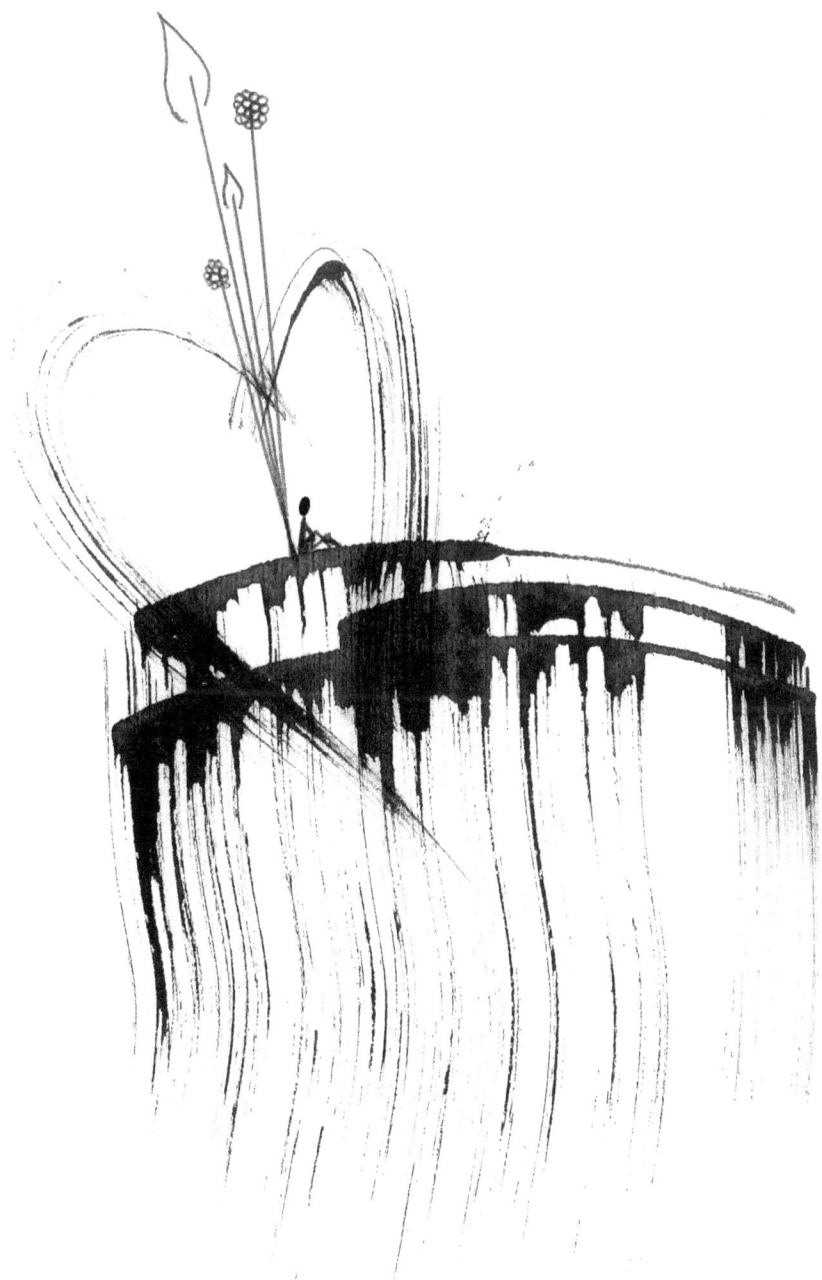

My heart of gold
And your troubled soul
Together they are stronger

I walk and I see
I laugh at all the signs, and I wait
Nothing happens until the day we will kiss again

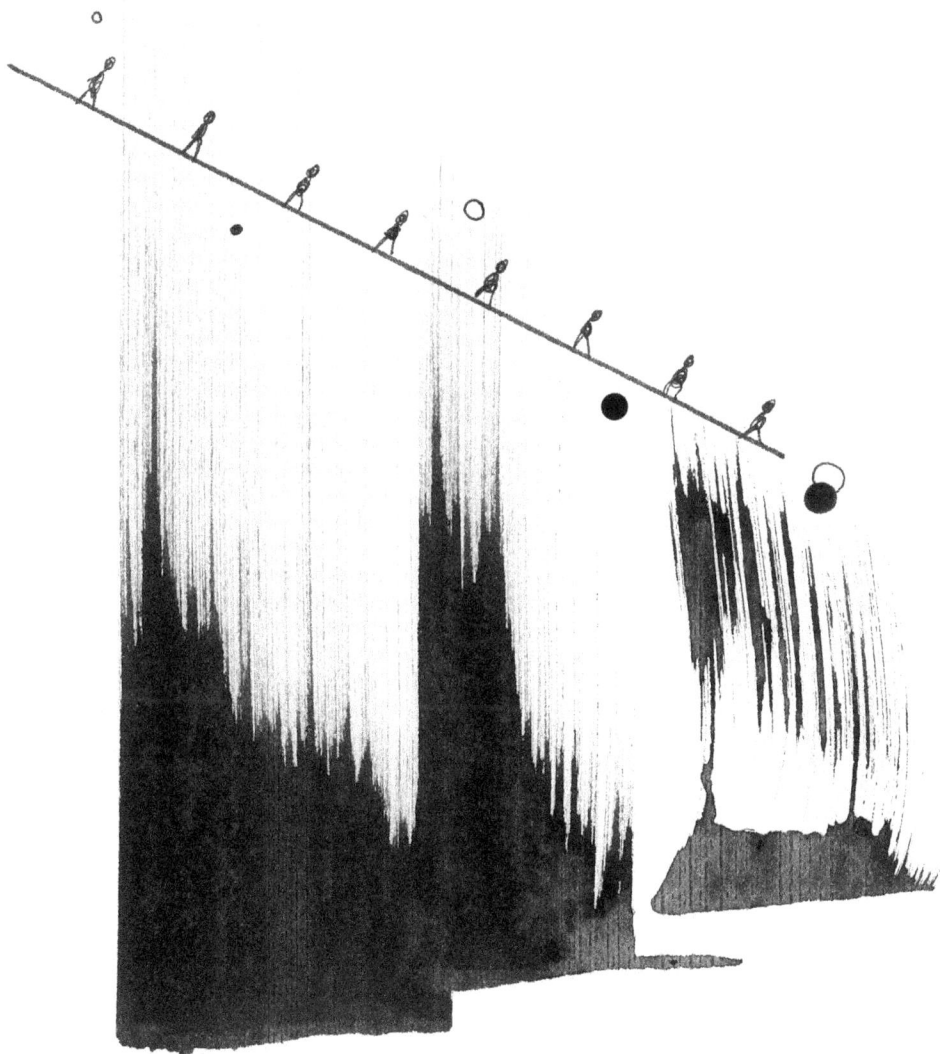

I have chosen you because you are funny
Laughing could save the world from a zombie apocalypse

The winter shores were so still
I met Avril
She told me to look at the sea glass
When I looked up, I saw your pain

You and I are like magnets
Why pull and push
When we can just lie in bed all day

Black and white are penguins
Grey is where we are now
Red is when our love ignites

Names can have meanings
Letters mean more
Ours match

Good or bad is not a train direction
Change tracks to find each other again

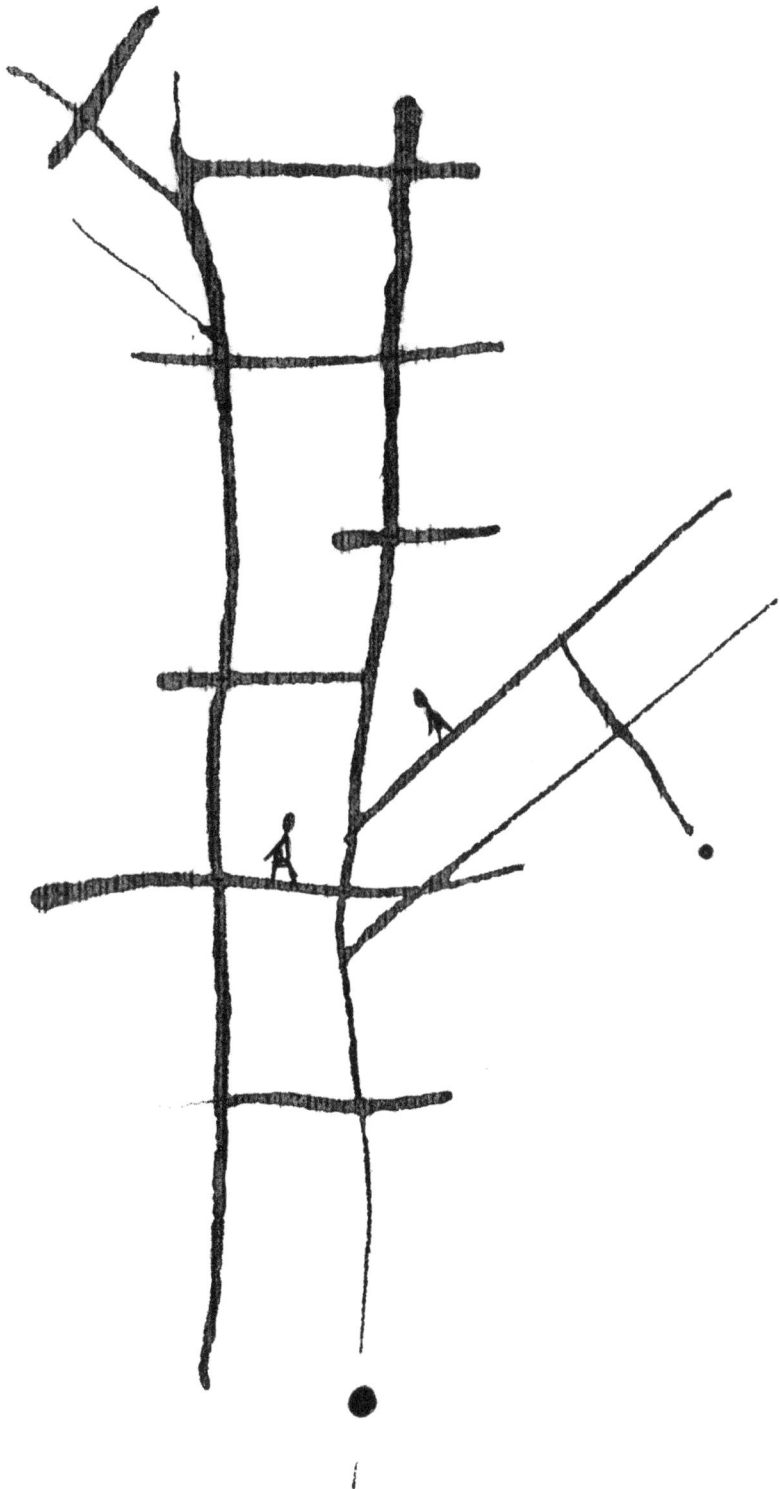

Are you the divine in a uniform?
You can take it off, but I still see you dressed
Shining

Bubbles in a bath hide a lot
Meanwhile the skin shrivels, and it reveals everything

Hasn't everyone had the one
If you haven't then you really should

Once upon a time on a Scottish coast
A secret wasn't worth keeping
It was worth screaming it from the hilltops

That's a nice back
I look around to understand
Only to realise the sharp pain you intended

Years and you still shy away
From knowing me more
From having it all

Hunt me down
Shoot me back
Never let me go

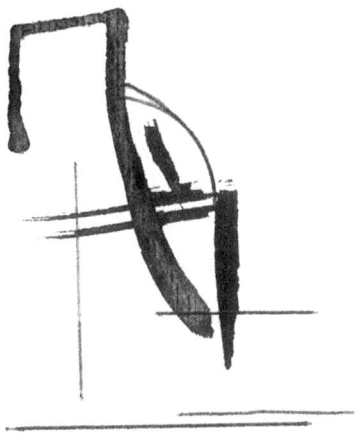

Pinkie swears are often broken
I wore mine like an armour
I am still wearing it while I wait
It is heavy

I understand
You
Full stop

Nuts can be allergic
Forests are a place I feel uneasy
Seeds are fun to watch grow
You are the sunshine in between my branches

Each minute apart feels like a 999 call
Long and desperate

Easy. That is a good word
Heartbeats slow down
Lips meet

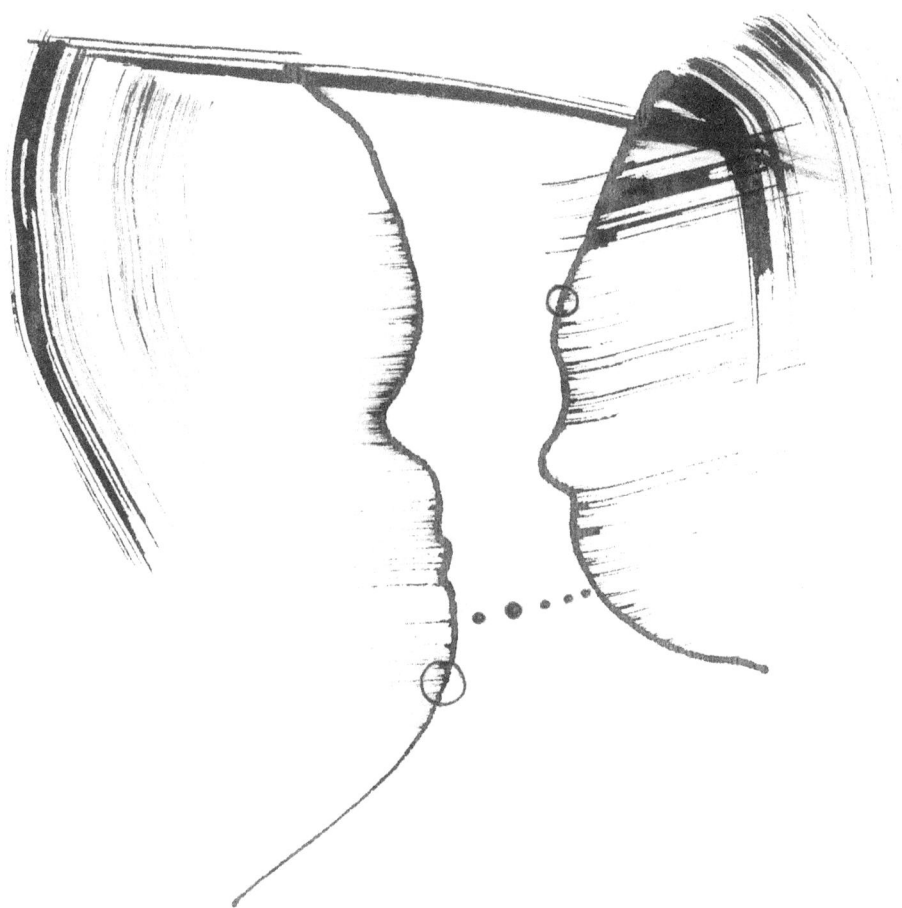

Does two really make sense
When it is us though a thousand times yes

How did I forget
There are years in between yesterday and today
Everyday my memories become clearer

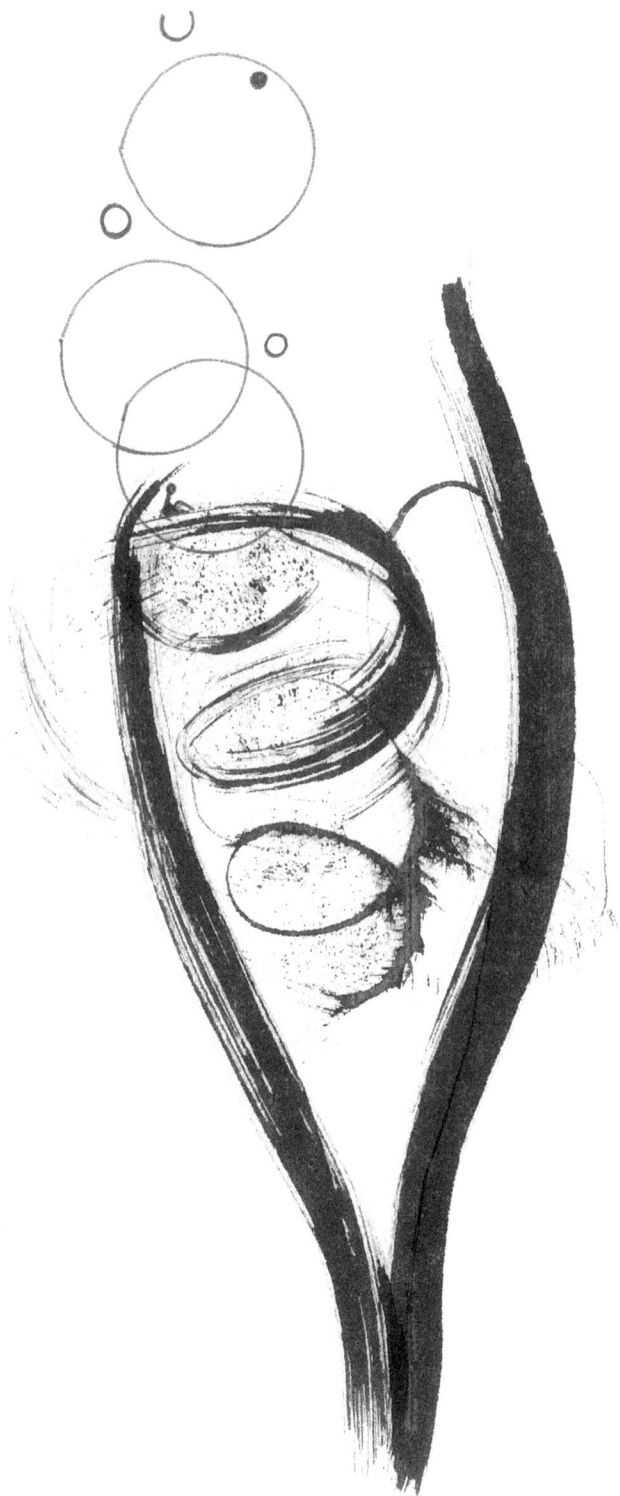

If I change my surname to yours
Our hearts will beat as one

Guidance down the right path
A wrong turn makes it juicy
But a bump seals the deal

You think it looks like a goat
I think it is a deer
If we look it up, we lose our spark

Who only buys one bottle of beer?
Someone who does not want to drink too much alone

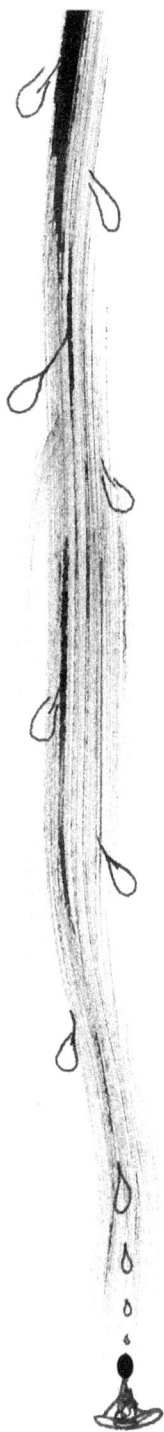

Your hands are tied with handcuffs you have created
Nothing can break them
I know I can

Silence is deafening
I heard everything you did not say

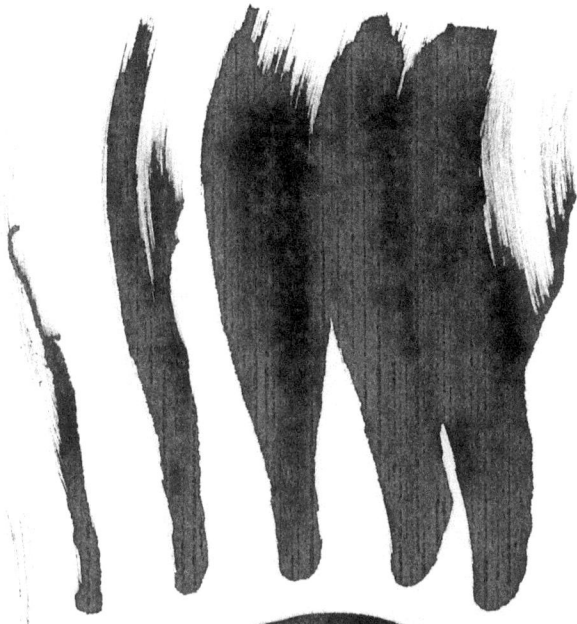

Young and free
Old and wise
Young and wise
Old and free

Two sides to every story
One side is upside down
The other is you and I together
And somehow that feels right

When the two right souls meet
The rest is out of their control

Distance is a strange concept
You are always near even if you choose not to be

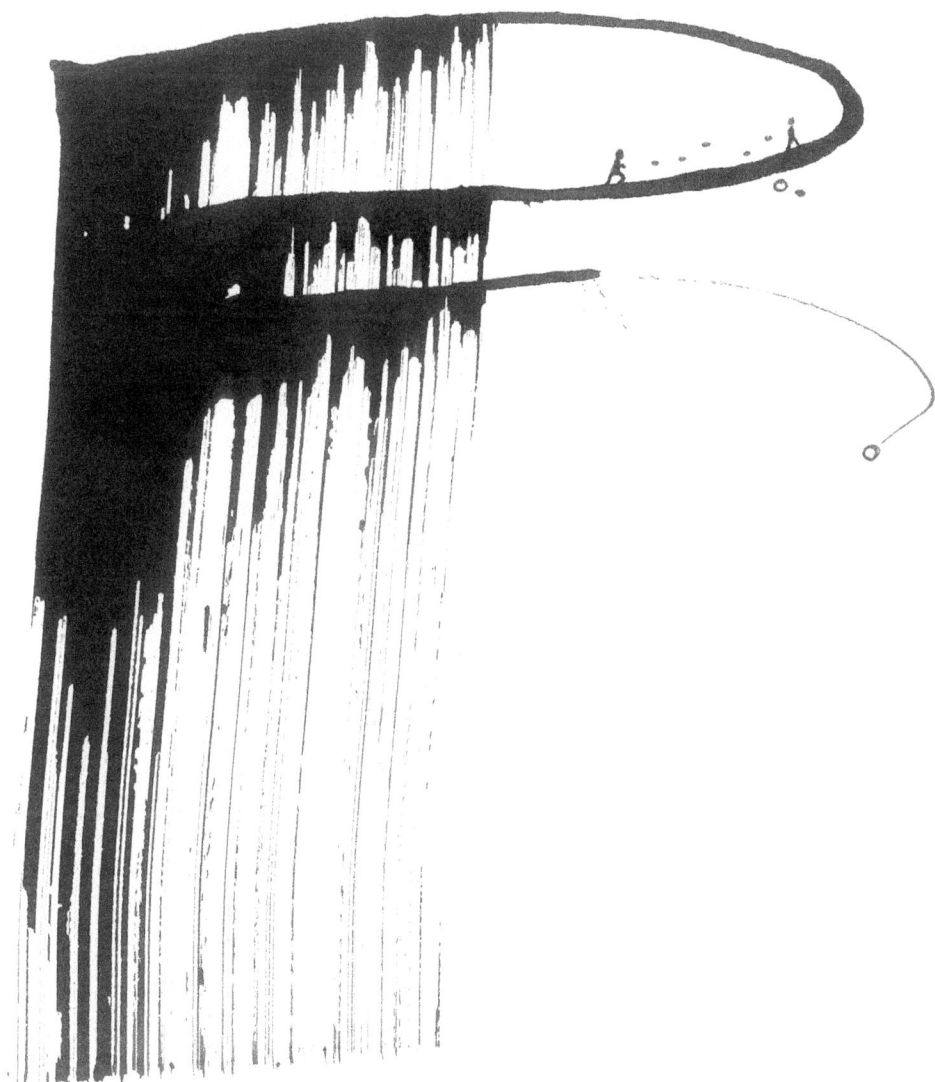

Without that look in your eyes
I would have walked past and never looked back

Together for a reason
Apart for none

Consistent

I am only that way because you allow me, to be me

I watched you watch the sun setting
What were you wishing for?

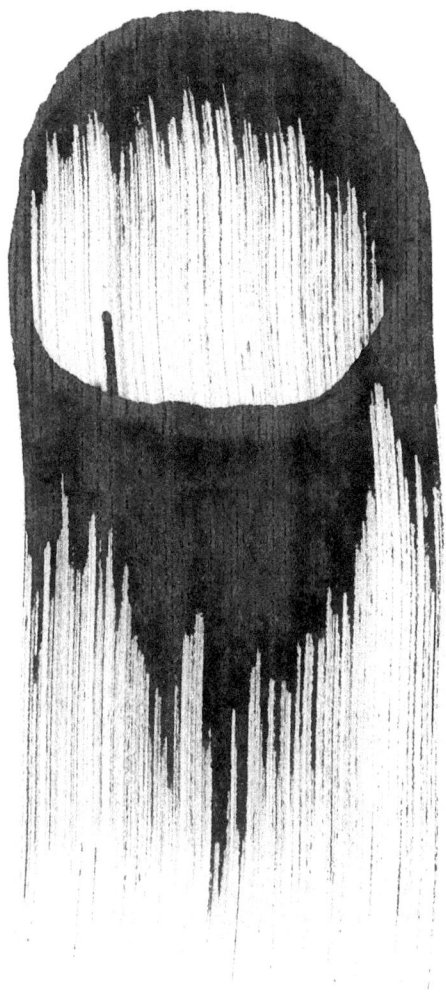

Spirits are there, I never knew
Your offering of half a clementine
Made me love you even more

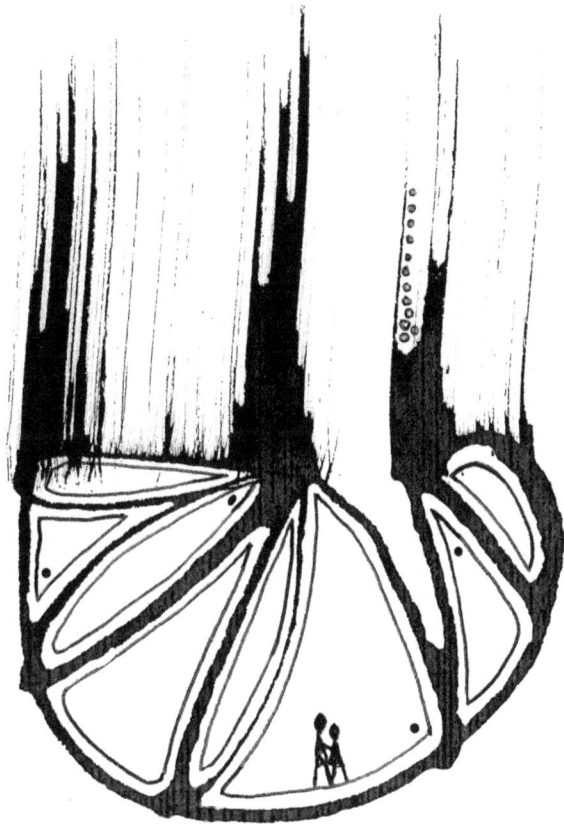